My Cat Saved My Life

My Cat Saved My Life

PHILLIP SCHREIBMAN

JEREMY P. TARCHER/PUTNAM
a member of Penguin Putnam Inc.
NEW YORK

Most Tarcher/Putnam books are available at special quantity discounts for bulk purchases for sales promotions, premiums, fund-raising, and educational needs. Special books or book excerpts also can be created to fit specific needs. For details, write Putnam Special Markets, 375 Hudson Street, New York, NY 10014.

Jeremy P. Tarcher/Putnam
a member of
Penguin Putnam Inc.
375 Hudson Street
New York, NY 10014
www.penguinputnam.com

Library of Congress Cataloging-in-Publication Data

Schreibman, Phillip, date.
My cat saved my life/Phillip Schreibman.—[1st American ed.].
p. cm.
ISBN 1-58542-063-8
1. Cat owners—Psychology. 2. Cats—Psychological aspects—Anecdotes.
3. Human-animal relationships—Anecdotes. 4. Schreibman, Phillip, date. I. Title.

SF442.86.S37   2000   00-041811
155.9'2—dc21

Cover Drawing: "Alice sleeping" © 1987 Phillip Schreibman

Printed in the United States of America

1   3   5   7   9   10   8   6   4   2

This book is printed on acid-free paper. ∞

For Alice, forever

Contents

cat *a small four-legged furry animal with a tail and claws, usually kept as a pet or for catching mice*

catalyst *an event or person that causes great change*

Introduction

This is a small story in the stories of the world. It's about a man and a cat and what the cat showed the man before it was too late. I was that man.

My whole life had come to a point, to a place, where finally my eyes could be opened. It was the culmination of years of despondency and confusion. I had painful memories and insoluble questions; and the sorrow from those memories and the terror of those questions had kept me down and broken my pride—that special human pride that would have prevented me from ever believing that I could learn the meaning of life from a cat.

That sounds funny. But by myself I had not done a very good job of figuring out life. Events had occurred which had shattered all my assumptions about what life was. I had fallen out of the rhythm of the world around me and could see no way to return.

But I had a bit of luck. I had a friend, a cat, named Alice. And she pulled me out of despair in the nick of time. She brought me back into the world. She saved my life.

Let me tell you the story:

1

Alley Cat

I met Alice about ten years ago in an alley near my house. The house was on a busy street in an immigrant, working-class section of Toronto. This was the spring of 1987 and the city was drying out from its usual grey bitter winter. As was I, or trying to, from a winter that had lasted almost a decade and still showed little sign of thawing.

It was a Saturday and I was in a deck chair in the backyard thinking of what to do with the rest of my life when my neighbour's son poked his head over the fence. A kitten, he said, had been coming to their door the past few evenings and maybe I wanted it and there it was in the alley right now.

I had had a cat, a crazy orange one, Charley, a stray who came to the back door one day and gradually moved in. Only two weeks before, he had been killed, beaten to death by a red-haired construction worker out on the street. My neighbour's son had found Charley's body and I guess he was trying to replace him in that way that kids look for justice. So, partly for the boy's sake, I went to have a look.

The kitten was in between two garages in the alley, frantically running up and down a dead-end, garbage-strewn passageway about half a foot wide. She was far too young to be out on her own and may have wandered away from the rest of a litter, or more probably had been abandoned by the owner. I wasn't sure I wanted another cat right then but she couldn't be left there. I decided I had better get her out.

The opening was too narrow for my body. I could put my arm in past the shoulder but not far enough to pick up the cat. Standing on the toes of one foot, holding in my breath and bending over, I rammed and squeezed between the sides of the garages until, by a stretch of the fingers, I could just reach the kitten. Suddenly, she backed down the passageway, climbing farther in through the piles of refuse and tin cans, all the while hissing and baring her teeth at me.

She looked wild and sort of terrifying. Which was crazy since she was only about seven inches long, maybe six weeks old, a tattered, ratty, striped tabby. The world around her, the cars speeding down the alley, the rush and bustle of this steel-and-concrete, self-absorbed city were all built to kill her. They had no room for her. Everything was stacked against her living another week.

But this cat didn't think she needed saving. I crouched down on the ground and called softly to her, trying all the known entreaties. Nothing I did could coax her to come within reach.

The day was getting hot and I was getting nowhere. My neighbour's son had left by this time and along came a little fat boy. He took one look at the kitten, decided to claim her, and ran off to ask his parents for permission to bring her home. I knew then for sure that I had to rescue this cat.

The boy lived in a house that bordered the bottom of our yard. His family had kept a dog outside in a wooden box for years. It was misshapen from being penned up. I had called the Humane Society but they would do nothing unless I made a formal complaint using my name in the process against these neighbours. Fearing retaliation against our own animals who frequented their yard, I did nothing. One day the dog was gone. I asked the boy what had happened to it and he said his father had told him that the dog was now working for the Toronto Transit Commission. I'm still not sure if that is a startlingly original euphemism for death or if I've been on that bus once or twice. Or both.

I ran home and got a saucer of milk, placed it just outside the crevice, and waited as the kitten approached to drink. When she got to the saucer, I reached down to grab her. And grabbed air. She had darted back into the passage before I knew my hand was empty. So I pressed close against a garage, out of sight. As she came out again, I leaped from my hiding place and, in a split-second move, swooped down, thrust out my arm, and missed. I tried again. And missed again. And again. It was a Saturday morning cartoon. I began to imagine someone watching from an upstairs window, laughing at this leaping idiot in the alley.

At last I surrendered and put the saucer inside the opening. The milk was gone in seconds; she was starving. How had she survived this long?

The alley was now baking hot. Out on the street, the Saturday traffic blared and growled. The sky was far away and empty. And down here it seemed lonesome: two specks in the grid of the city, man and cat, in an obscure little drama. I felt desperate. The little fat boy would be back any minute.

Out of nowhere came another kid. Maybe he was the one who had been laughing at me. "You trying to catch this cat?" he says. And he bent over in the alley, sifting through the gravel, and came up with a dirty old piece of string. Then he began to dangle and snake this string along the ground in front of the passageway. He was fishing for cat.

And here came the kitten, starved, scared, lonely, and helpless—but now the huntress, moving slowly, with knees bent and tail flicking, all seven inches, paw by paw, to stalk the wild string. She had put aside all troubles to come and play the cat. When her concentration was at its fullest and she had batted at the string a couple of times, I snatched her up.

4

Like a little Tasmanian devil, she struggled and hissed at me while I carried her back to the house. There, fumbling key and cat and saucer, I managed to get the door open, set everything down inside, and slam it shut. When I turned around, the kitten had disappeared.

For half an hour I scoured the house from top to bottom but there wasn't a whisker of her. I had to go out to rehearsal so I left a note for Mary:

> *There's a kitten somewhere in the house.*
> *I don't know if we should keep it.*

When Mary came home and saw the note, she searched all over for the cat with no better luck. Finally giving up, she sat down to read. About two hours later, long after Mary had completely forgotten about it, the kitten marched into the room, looking, Mary told me, "like she owned the place."

Indeed she did. There seemed to be no question of whether to "keep it." She had decided to stay. Alice had joined her life with ours, and now my fate and time were bound up with a force and a soul which would leave me changed forever. Changed as a human, as an animal, as a piece of creation.

2

The Situation

Here I must explain the situation that Alice had walked into. It was not a particularly pleasant one. My life was in a state of suspended animation, a kind of mental and emotional paralysis that had begun with the death of my father, eight years earlier, and had gotten worse after my mother died, about two years before I met Alice. Despite the time that had passed, I could not seem to shake off the effects of those deaths.

I had seen my parents die at the end of lengthy and terrible illnesses. I had tried what I could to save them and I had failed. They died slowly, in great physical and mental pain, and it was a hard thing to witness.

We are supposed to be prepared for such things. We know that each of our lives will be touched by death, some perhaps more than others, and eventually we will face our own. Yet I am sure mine will be easier than having to watch helplessly the death of someone I love.

Still, it was not only the distress and sorrow which I felt for my parents' deaths that had affected me. It was the moment of death itself.

At each of their hospital beds, six years apart, I saw the last breath of their lives leave their bodies. And as I sat there, it appeared that what separated them from being the man and woman I had known all my life was the shortest span of time in the universe. A miracle of experiences, hopes, stories, thoughts, a way of smiling, a voice, vanished in the smallest fraction of a second.

In an instant, an impenetrable wall blocked me from their presence. There was only emptiness here where all that life that was in them had been. On the other side was the mystery I had heard about, read about, thought about, but had never before truly felt. Now, all the parts of me where my day-to-day living had once entwined with theirs were reaching out into nothing. In a flash of absolute clarity, I was made completely conscious of the power, the terror, the blankness of death.

The physical body of my parent was lying in front of me but there was no one inside it. I could not comprehend where the person had gone to. It had been torn out by a force without form or face. Only the energy of this force was visible: in the struggle that the dying had made against it. And they had been as powerless as we who remained behind, sitting amongst the doctors and their machines, and with all our love radiating out into infinity. Everything had just stopped.

It was a scene of cold horror and I did not want to admit to what I was looking at. For my parents' deaths had given me a glimpse into a void even greater than the one that they had left in my life, and it terrified me. Death had unveiled the reality we try so desperately in our daily lives to avoid seeing: *we know nothing*.

It was as if a mist had been permanently removed from in front of my eyes. For what did we really know? Only that we are in a situation. We call it life. In our minds, we create a world where sciences, philosophies, religions all offer up explanations for this situation. We accept one or more of them and carry on living.

At that moment in the hospital room I could observe the workings of the explanations: nurses bustled about; doctors arrived to confirm the obvious; relatives wept and soon began to discuss funeral arrangements. Outside in the street there was the continuing rumble of traffic. The world carried on.

It appeared as a charade, a play of make-believe that ignored the blunt reality of what had just occurred. Someone I loved had disappeared off the face of the earth. There was no explanation. It was a farce.

Yet the world expected that I keep up my part in its show and, after my father's funeral, I did try to get back into character, to return to normal daily life. But when I said my lines, they had no feeling; I didn't believe in the script. And on the death of my mother, it was soon apparent that my ability to act in this play was totally gone. The concerns and ambitions of human society seemed fatuous. Cars, buildings, people; career, love, relationships; all had no relevance. The world had split open and revealed the void in all its inexplicability.

I did not want to contemplate this void yet I could not forget it. The experience of witnessing my parents' deaths would not be erased. I was stranded at the cross-roads, without signposts or map, in a place where I knew *we know nothing*, but could see no way of carrying on my life with that realization. And tangled up in my bewilderment was the grief for those deaths.

I fell into this grief. It wasn't difficult; my mother and father were quite wonderful people. I had loved them and I missed having them here. I wept a great deal for my loss and for the sorrow and injustice in their lives and deaths. But after a time, after each death, I found it necessary to curtail my mourning because the grieving seemed to have no end.

There is a kind of crying, a howling really, that is like going down a long dark hallway. You expect to see some light under the door at the end, but there is no door. The corridor is endless. There is no release, no catharsis. The crying could go on forever.

Eventually you have to put the tears aside, physically stop them. You must do your work, cook meals, pay bills, function in the world. But you are still in that hallway. You have stopped looking for the door; you have even forgotten all about your search. The sorrow becomes a part of you, a heaviness in you. In this state you continue to act: in a condition of arrested grief.

That is where I was stuck when I met Alice. Confused among people, angry at trifles, depressed and distracted in all my endeavours, I saw the world through this heaviness. A crazy fear came over me that anyone I loved would die; my relationships with those close to me began to suffer.

My mind was dazed and my body, a distant haze; I did not seem to occupy any space. This body of mine was only a conveyance, a backpack stuffed with my dumbfounded brain, both carried about by a ghost. The experience of these deaths resulted in my shrinking from life. I did not care to be a living creature.

Although I had made a pretence of going along with the game for awhile, it all caught up with me. I had been a composer; ultimately, I stopped wanting to write music. At the age of 39, my life ground to a halt.

I was in rough shape. And so was Alice.

3

A Fine Mess

Physically, Alice was a mess. She was dehydrated and malnourished. Her ears were infested with mites. Her eyes were running from a chronic infection. Worst of all, she had a hernia which protruded from her tiny body like a golf ball.

We took her to our vet who said an operation was imperative but possibly fatal. She was so small and weak that she could die simply from the anaesthetic. So, in order to improve her chances of surviving it, the procedure was delayed a few weeks while her strength could be built up.

We have a videotape of Alice from those weeks. In the background can be heard Mary talking on the telephone, making final arrangements for the surgery. And on the screen is Alice, digging her teeth into my hand and then pouncing on it. (They were about the same size.) Sick as she was, Alice was taking on the world.

She was a little powerhouse. She ran, played, climbed trees, and explored the backyard as if nothing were wrong with her. Just as she had attacked the string in the alley, nothing in her condition was going to stop her from getting on with the job of becoming a cat.

She leaped into this task. In fact she leaped at everything, jumping many times her own height at any of the toys we dangled over her. Her body would swirl into the air, flashing like a salmon on its way upstream, and then land breathing hard, with her head up, calculating the next attempt. She was tireless, literally jumping for joy, and in the display of her heroic feats, the courage and ardour of her efforts, she had begun to leap into our hearts as well.

But I eyed her with the wariness of a potential mourner. Not knowing if she could endure the surgery, wondering how long we would know her, I stayed back a little ways from Alice. I was not about to make another painful connection.

On the day before the operation, Mary and I stood in the back room, looking out into the yard. We were watching Alice, out in the sunny afternoon, springing on a branch of the apricot tree and sniffing at the few remaining blossoms. In a few minutes we would be leaving for the vet's, and we had to go out and pluck Alice out of the tree, out of the afternoon, and take her.

I wondered aloud to Mary if maybe we shouldn't take the kitten to the clinic after all. Perhaps she should just live out the amount of time she had left, instead of dying the next morning on an operating table. Let her have a few more weeks or days or whatever had been decided for her.

In the end, we decided: we couldn't deny the little kitten the chance to become a cat. We drove Alice to the clinic and dropped her off. And the house seemed empty when we got back. Despite me, she had made a space there.

Next day we waited out the hours, past the time when the surgery should have been over, and finally made the nervous phone call: we learned that we still had a future cat. Alice had made it through.

We went to the clinic to pick her up. Jack, our vet, met us at the front desk, smiling. He told us that when he had finished stitching her up, Alice looked like she had a zipper going the length of her body, as if she were someone in a cat suit. "Shhh," said Jack, putting his finger to his lips. "Don't tell anyone."

Out of the back room came Jack's assistant, Robin, carrying an impossibly small bundle of fur—already smaller in person than I remembered her presence—and handed Alice over to me.

I put her in the fold of my arm. With a tiny exhalation of breath, she lay her head against my chest. It was such an unmistakable expression of relief that, amid the "oohs" and "aahs" that now arose in the waiting room, I realized that this little life had made a connection to me, despite me.

4

The Connection

I had not ceased trying to make a connection to the world. Constantly I had been searching for ways out of my predicament.

I read self-help books and books about depression and about death and the stages of grief. My symptoms were recognizable in them but they had contained no solutions to my disease. The authors all related their remedies to a world of which I no longer felt part.

A friend suggested psychotherapy and therapeutic drugs, and I considered them once again. Years before, when circumstances made coping difficult, I had tried these methods without lasting success. After any of the treatments ended, life loomed up again. They proved to be closed systems which only delayed dealing with the essential questions. Bandages for lethal wounds, they got me up and running; but all that running had gotten me nowhere.

Now there was nowhere to run. I had no choice but to try and figure this out. My concern with death led me naturally to works of philosophy and religion and mysticism. And through reading them, I realized that I had removed myself from God.

It was not so much that I was a nonbeliever. Something in the Jewish tradition I had been raised in had made the idea of a Creator an indestructible part of my outlook. I felt there was a First Cause to all of this; we will argue for eternity about what name to call it.

The Deity I had grown apart from was the One who was supposed to watch over me and answer my prayers and yet had allowed the suffering and the agonizing deaths I had witnessed. If God were intervening in history, it was not my history. And if there was a reason behind the suffering—a punishment or retribution—it did not seem to fit the crime. Divine justice appeared to have no logic and I was not able to make up excuses for it anymore.

I had withdrawn from my relationship with the God of my childhood—more out of disappointment than disbelief—but I was still drawn to the Creator. If there were explanations to be found, it would be here. I had to begin again in the beginning.

I decided to explore the Kabbalah, the mystical teachings at the core of my own religion. Since I knew very little Hebrew and no Aramaic, my reading was confined to interpretations and translations of the original texts. I accepted that I was at a disadvantage; each writer had his or her own slant on the subject. Nonetheless, there was for me an immediate connection. Common to all the books were realistic probings of the questions that were closest to my heart: all shared an acceptance of the mystery of existence.

The usual explanations were avoided. The Kabbalists acknowledged that at the centre was the Unknowable. All we could ever comprehend was what was here, in what they called *Creation*. And if we fully realized it, if we were totally in the place of *Creation*, then we would be connected to the Creator.

Now I felt drawn to the idea of *Creation*, this point of connecting, but once again I was at a disadvantage. The Kabbalists spent years of study in the original languages to learn various methods of prayer, using meditation, even music and weeping, in order to achieve the proper state of being in *Creation*. I was a novice, a dilettante who lacked even the basic firm grounding in the world that the Kabbalah said was necessary to approach this study. It demanded that you have humility and I was too self-obsessed. The place it spoke of, what it called *Creation*, could only be an intellectual concept to me. In my state, there was no chance of a direct experience.

I was stymied; I needed something, a link, and I did not know how I would ever find it or even what it was.

5

Alice Moves In

A lice moved in and took over the house. She was small and everywhere. Any hand left unattended was attacked. Pant legs were ascended; knees, beseiged; shoes were wrestled and subdued. Our hallway turned into a racetrack and the back of the couch was now a launching pad.

Suddenly, *everything* was interesting. Unassuming corners of coats, tables, and books became regions of mystery and indefatigable attention. A fly was astounding. A flower was a universe. Alice was figuring out the world.

I remember at this time we had a Purim party at our house with a few friends over. A table low to the floor had been set for the dinner with cushions arranged about to sit on, a real Persian banquet. We had decided to make a videotape of the celebration and the camera was put at the head of the table. After I made sure that everyone sitting around would be in the picture, we all left the room to prepare the rest of the food. When we viewed the videotape later, I realized that I had inadvertently left the camera running the whole time we were gone. For about fifteen minutes, there was a still-life picture of the table settings: coloured napkins, candles, wine bottles, plates, and glasses; fish, salads, breads, and cakes—and then a little face came into view.

It was Alice. She had never been to a party before. Her face was alight with excitement and expectation. She went all around the table, looking and looking, her eyes wide, her head turning back and forth among all the strange new things. But she never touched the food; the little cat already had a perfect instinct for the proper decorum at a party.

It was a situation of great privilege to see a young creature in its first encounters with life. To her, nothing was taken for granted. All was remarkable. Simply witnessing the explosion of energy was inspiring. In a way, I was myself given a chance to start over, to look at everything with new eyes, ears, and nose. What Alice was experiencing in this strange new place, the world, could have been a catalyst for my own fresh appreciation of life.

As luck would have it, soon after Alice's operation, I became embroiled in a lawsuit with a large Canadian corporation in order to recover unpaid music royalties. The time-consuming legal wrangling lasted two years. Consequently, I missed a lot of Alice's growing up.

Not that Alice could go unnoticed. But I saw her development not as a smooth continuous film—more like a series of snapshots. First, she got very square. Her parts were stocky and she moved around like a small jeep. Then she was all legs, stretching them out in a tangle when she fell asleep on a chair. Her ears got smaller, her eyes swept out to the sides like an Egyptian princess, and suddenly I realized she was very beautiful.

It was at this age, all legs and stripes and eyes, that she ran wild in the neighbourhood. On summer evenings, in the early darkness, when the smells of the grass and earth were overwhelming, her lips would become red and spots like rouge appeared on her cheeks. She disappeared into the garden and leaped across the fences. In the moonlight, we could see her outline on the pitch of the row of garages in the alley, high-stepping from peak to peak, dancing on the rooftops.

A new sound came over the neighbourhood: Alice's name echoing through the nights of warm, redolent air (Cat Nights, we called them) when Mary stood in the backyard and cried: *"A—li—ce!"* like a call to prayer, to the comfort of remembering that she existed, that her presence and atmosphere were in the world.

We lost her a few times in those days. Posters were printed and pasted on hydro poles in the nearby streets, with promise of great reward for the safe return of our striped wanderer. But she always came back on her own. She had to. I needed her even if I did not yet know it.

6

The Wall

There was another layer to my situation, an attitude of mind which had come over me so gradually and subtly that I was ignorant of its presence, and which now hampered my attempts to connect back into the world. It was a condition made all the more insidious because I had invited it.

When my mother was suffering from her long illness—she was eleven months in hospital—I would receive phone calls almost daily from doctors reporting the results of her medical tests, discussing her prognosis, or alerting me to a new crisis in her disease. At that time I was writing music for episodes of a television show on a tight schedule. The phone would ring and it was usually bad news. Many times I was required to make instant decisions regarding the course of my mother's treatment: matters of life and death. After these calls, I had to continue writing in order to meet my deadlines. Each evening I visited her and saw her pain and terror firsthand. Then I returned home to come up with some more music for this comedy series.

The particularly leaden atmosphere of hospitals was familiar to me. My mother had been in them often; and when I was eighteen, I myself had spent a month in one. I remember that New Year's Eve occurred during my stay, and my mother came to spend it with me in that pale green room. She asked if there were something she could get me and I couldn't think of anything but that she should get me out of there. Then I recalled how it had been weeks since I had played any music. Without imagining that it was even remotely possible, I said that I would like nothing better at that moment than to play a piano.

She never questioned my request though it must have been a bizarre one to the nurses on duty. Instead, she left me the nail clippers from her purse to ready my fingers, and searched the darkened and semi-deserted hospital for over an hour. Finally, after trudging out through the snow, she found a piano in a nearby nurses' residence.

Of course, they wouldn't let me play it. The only music my mother and I heard that night was the distant bell of the town clock striking midnight. But my mother had understood what I needed and she had spared no energy to try and help me.

It was typical of her. She had the most kind and compassionate nature I have ever known. Her generosity was legendary. She ran her own ladies' wear business in our town, and newly arrived Polish immigrants would come to her store and leave not only with bags of free clothing but with gifts of money as well. As busy as she was, there was always time to hear any hard-luck story that came her way and to help however she could.

Now I was witnessing the reward for a lifetime of kindness: a slow death in a stark room filled with the tubing and medical paraphernalia of a science that could neither seem to heal her nor let her go. I desperately wanted to help her, save her, get her out of there. But if I were going to be of any use, I needed a clear and calm mind.

To brace myself for the doctors' phone calls and the hospital visits, I began to develop a distancing mechanism which would reduce the shock of whatever new horror was awaiting. Some part of me heard and saw everything, but before it could register emotionally. This allowed me to cope with the doctors and the fear for my mother's life; and to hold down my job by keeping a separate place inside myself from where I could draw out the music.

What began as a mechanism became a reflex and a mindset. Always on high alert, nerves in extreme tension, I waited to ward off the next blow. The distancing between myself and events as they were occurring was active constantly. Like the time delay on a radio talk show, everything was screened out and censored before it reached me.

And when my mother died, this mechanism did not disappear. If anything, it got worse. No longer aware it was there, I thought this was life. No experience was happening in real time. It was being displayed on a screen for analysis. I had set up a DEW line, an early warning system around myself, which I could not shut off.

An invisible wall surrounded me, impermeable to the world. But a wall has to be pretty high to keep a cat out.

7

Cat Habits

Alice and I began to live beside each other. Imperceptibly, as we shared the same time and space, she infiltrated my life. No matter that I was distracted or brooding; Alice insisted on my attention. I could not avoid her. Before I knew it, we had habits together and my days became her days as well.

Every morning, really early, she woke me up. She sprang onto the night table and knocked a pencil off or, in extremity, the alarm clock, the sound of which hitting the floor never failed to get me out of bed. In the semidarkness, I shuffled downstairs behind her into the kitchen. There, she assumed a position in the centre of the floor, erect, with her back to me. This was the signal for *"Where's the grub?"* My hands, still thick with sleep, grappled with the can opener. I would set down her dish, make myself a coffee, and so we would have breakfast together.

While I showered, she always waited outside the bathroom door, calling to me or shoving a paw under to remind me she was there. Her body would be so tight up against it, her mouth pressed to the opening, that I began pushing the door open cautiously, slowly, not to bump her—a habit I still have.

She visited me in the basement music studio, leaping onto my lap and lying under my hands while I played, sometimes even taking a stroll across the keyboard in an atonal mode. Or if I was stuck indoors at my desk, making endless phonecalls and sorting through bills and files, she brought the news from outside.

First, she announced herself from the doorway and I, inevitably engrossed in some picayune detail, would mutter, "Just a minute, Alice." Then she sat down in the office, waiting just at the corner of my vision, while I continued to struggle with my banal tasks, all the while trying to ignore her.

Tense minutes would trickle by until finally, losing all patience, Alice would spring onto the desk, smack in the middle of my papers, and stick the world under my nose: fresh snow, bits of leaves, the smell of the cedar trees in her fur.

Work was now out of the question. I followed her to the back door to see what was so urgent. Usually it was a bird in a branch or a sudden summer downpour; maybe the first slow fall of heavy snowflakes had come or a burst of midwinter sunshine was floodlighting the yard. I had ceased paying attention to these things.

Alice would be crying at the back door. *Why didn't she use the cat door, for chrissakes?* Irritably, I would fling it open. Then the two of us, man and cat, would stand there for awhile together in the open doorway as the rain-filled air, some flakes of snow, or the sound of the bird would meet my face directly, despite me.

At some point in the day, Alice would come and get me just to have a game. When I left my desk to follow her, she would suddenly pick up speed and, with a whoop, race down the hall and hide behind a door. When I came abreast of the door, she would leap out, attack my shoe, and tear off to the next hiding place, under a couch or in a box.

I couldn't remember the last time I had played hide-and-seek or tag or any game for that matter. The idea of play was no longer part of my life. But Alice had to get a game going every day and she wouldn't leave me alone until we had one.

And once she got me going, huffing and puffing around the house and chasing her up and down the stairs, she had gotten not only my blood moving, but she had moved my spirit as well. I felt light-headed. We were engaged in a mindless pursuit, trying to catch each other, and for awhile each day that was all I was thinking about.

Each night she got on the bed and lay beside me, leaning her weight against my leg. She was just out of reach, like in the alley that first day. But this time I could stretch out my hand and graze her fur.

We lay there together in the darkness while the city traffic continued to roar outside. Car alarms went off; sirens screamed by; streetcars shook the house.

My mind was roaring too: with all the angers and sorrows and fears that had plagued me during the day. But something in her presence made a stillness settle on the room. My mind would calm down a little and the memories would shut off for awhile. And as my eyes adjusted to the dark, I could just make out her shape at the bottom of the bed.

There was a kind of clarity to this image that broke through to me. Here, amongst the shadows of the heavy furniture, we were simply two beings in a room. Only that. Then, for the briefest of moments, I was there with her. For a tiny instant, I was no longer living in my mind but in the room.

I know it was Alice being in the room that brought me there. I felt safe. After all, she was a cat; she sought out only the best places. So if Alice were here, it was all right. Her shape in the darkness was like an amulet.

Night after night I tried to practise coming out of hiding, venturing into the place where Alice was. Sometimes, for split seconds, I had a glimpse of some-where that existed outside myself: the spot that was just here in the room with Alice.

I realized that Alice was always in the room. I was living in a spot about two inches above my head, watching.

8
The Job

Death had put me in that spot. I was watching out for him. But Alice managed to pull me down a couple of inches into the business and bustle of her life. So I began to watch her.

And as I watched Alice, it became obvious that she was doing a better job of living than I was. To her, each day held promise from the moment the clock hit the floor until the last call in the yard and the final closing time of the cat door. Everything she did in between was approached with full energy—and even the sleeping afterwards had a purposeful intensity to it.

Alice had an intensity about her. There was a thoughtfulness in her actions and demeanour, a confidence and dignity of manner. There was always something on her mind.

She set about her life with seriousness and a surety of purpose. Not without humour, but with concentration and optimism, Alice was actively pursuing her career. And although I had not thought of cats as having a career, in fact, they do. Living is their career.

This may sound self-evident and coy. After all, aren't we all engaged in living? However, I did not know anyone who was content with just "living." Everyone seemed to need something to live *for* or to make living "worthwhile": the Good Life.

Not so with a cat. Being, as a cat, is their sole occupation and they work hard at perfecting the skills to get the job done right.

I imagined a sort of Feline Finishing School. Each cat sets about with its raw materials to have a life: gathers to itself arms, legs, fur, ears, grows a nose, cultivates a tail, has meetings with other cats, learns a few choice sturdy words (no need for too many), studies Squirrel, makes sleeping into an art, and fine-tunes the mechanism that reaches into the human heart.

Alice reached into mine. When she entered the room, it eased a little. I began to look forward to just being around her. There was a contagion to her optimism; she was a walking advertisement for life. Whatever Alice was doing to figure out the mystery of getting along in the world, it worked.

Perhaps it could work for me as well—if only I could learn her technique. And so I fell under the influence of Alice's outlook and decided to become her student.

9

A Person

Placing myself under Alice's tutelage sealed forever the change that was already occurring in our relationship. It had become apparent to me for some time that Alice did not think of herself as a domestic cat. Rather, she regarded herself as another person in the household and expected to be treated as such. After a few years of our hanging out together, she succeeded in convincing me of that fact: she was a person.

This is difficult for a cat to do. For one thing, they're short. From way down there they have to work hard to get the message up through all that altitude. But hardest to get through is the attitude. After all, she was on four legs; I was on two. I was a human; she was my pet. I owned her. And as a human, I merited *respect*, *loyalty*, *adoration*, etc. She could be "cute" and "cuddly," maybe even "pesky" or "dratted," but where did she come off being a person? She was an *ANIMAL*.

I did not think of myself as an animal. All my life I had heard it as a term of abuse, a put-down. *A brutish person* is one dictionary definition. On the other hand, to be human is to be *kind, considerate,* or even *humane*— like the organizations we create to take care of animals abused and abandoned by "humans."

I could see that condescension and prejudice towards other animals were embedded in our language like sexist terminology. The human race was racist on a species scale. To us, only a human could have the characteristics of a person, could be an individual with feelings, appreciation, uniqueness, a soul. Yet Alice's behaviour displayed all of these attributes. She had a personality— of huge and varied dimension.

At this time, another cat, a thin grey stray named Chico, came to live with us. Alice made it clear she was none too elated at sharing the house with anyone else. There was no outright hostility to Chico: more of a sulky resignation to the inevitability of his continued residence. That made it all the more remarkable to see her reaction when Chico returned after a night at the vet's. She met him at the door, solicitously touched noses to make sure everything was okay, and welcomed him back into the house. Her attitudes were complex.

She evinced them with the means at her disposal: the physical limitations of her body. Since I was accustomed to only the human clues, coming from language, costume, stance, facial expressions, and hand movements, the manifestation of her personality was subtle.

For example, Alice's sense of humour had to be understood on cat terms. She played tricks. She loved hiding on Mary and suddenly jumping out from behind doors and out of closets and scaring her. It never failed to evoke a squeal from Mary, and then Alice would stroll away very, very slowly. Her walk was like Jack Benny's, a deadpan gesture to top her punch line.

One time while holding Alice on her lap, Mary, in a whimsical mood, placed her mouth around Alice's snout. Alice drew back for a moment, in a double-take, and then, with exquisite timing, reached up her face and very gently bit down on Mary's nose.

And when we tried to get Alice indoors at night, she would return to the sound of our calling, but sit tauntingly on the other side of the fence, just out of reach. From there she stared back languidly while we pleaded with her to come home. We even put cat candies through the fence, trying to tempt her over. These she delicately swallowed; then she moved a little further away. Finally we would give up and go back in the house. Seconds later, bursting through the cat door, Alice would race by us and up the stairs to bed. When we got there, she would be pretending to be asleep.

Making jokes, practical and otherwise, is an activity that we associate particularly with being human. We guard jealously our ability to create humour out of events. A sense of humour denotes a perspective on things, a conceptual distance or an ironic stance; it means that the Jokester has a philosophy of life. Having a philosophy is not something we will readily ascribe to animals. It makes them too much like people.

I had always been suspicious of pet owners who treated their animals as people. It seemed that they were projecting a "person-ness" onto them out of their own imaginations and desires. Yet, in order to get along in society, I had had to create and then project a personality on myself. How much of a personality does anyone manufacture in order to function at his or her job, be the life of the party, or dress up in fancy clothes? Most of the time we are the selves we want others to see.

It seemed to me that we humans were simply self-conscious animals. And by withholding this concept of "self" from other animals, we maintained our position of superiority over them. From this pinnacle it was easier for us to control, experiment on, and kill them.

The same idea, as the Nazis knew so well, could be applied to human beings. Destroy their sense of being a person, and their ability to resist is impaired. Make them "nonpersons," and you can do what you want to them with a clear conscience. This has been done to our co-animals. We have defined them and put them in their place: under our thumbs (and under our belts).

Alice did not see things this way. She went about her life with no regard for any differences between humans and cats. And as she and I shared our lives, had mutual experiences and common memories, as our habits formed into routines of living and we became part of each other, I could see no difference either.

Like any relationship, the physical appearance of the Other had become secondary. I no longer saw a cat; I did not notice fur, whiskers, and paws. Before me was another unfathomable soul on the earth. My human bias faded away and now I began to interact with Alice as a person and as an equal.

I can remember when it occurred to me that Alice's relationship to humans was not one of subservience. Whenever I arrived home, she would always come to meet me at the front door. After I greeted her with "*Hi, Alice!*" she would turn around, stretch out her front paws, and raise her back end up high in the air towards me. One day it finally dawned on me that this visual pun was plain English for "*Hi, asshole!*"

I was not insulted. It was the admonition of a Zen master. I *was* being an asshole. My mind was filled only with the tired movie of my life which I was running and rerunning over and over again, trying to figure out what had happened to me. The film was getting chewed up in the projector while I could see nothing else of what was all around me.

I lived my days in a benumbed passivity. Nothing I had done had worked. My pride was broken. All of my self-images had been shattered. I no longer had a conception of myself as particularly anybody or anything. Being "human" was irrelevant.

I was ready for cat school.

10

Mary's Story

Mary once said that she figured all the animals got together to have a meeting where they discussed what to do about humans. We were wrecking everything and making their lives miserable. The solution everyone agreed upon was that one animal had to go and live with us and show us the proper way to be. The elephant was too big and the snake had gotten a bad reputation. The dog had already tried but he was too softhearted. Everyone had an excuse.

The cat was pretending to be asleep, but soon got tired of listening to all the arguing.

"Okay, okay," she said. "I'll go. I guess I'm probably the most cynical of all of you. Only someone with a refined sense of irony could live among those poor *kuckers*★. But one thing," and here she raised her eyebrows and a paw, "I don't fetch."

★stinkers

11

Cat School

M ost of what I learned from Alice came about by observing her and following her around. I let myself be subject to her will. If she wanted me to come somewhere, I went with her. I looked for her signals. I looked at things she looked at.

And I tried not to get impatient with the length of time that she took to look at them. I wanted to realize what there was about each activity that was important to her strategy of life. (What *was* she doing there in the window?) To be sure, a lot of it was cat communication and vigilance. But some of it was something else.

I watched her negotiate the twists and turns of living, how she went about things, how she moved her body around. And in this, she was making me aware of *my* body. A cat is firmly rooted in the physical world; having a body was the link, the relationship to all else. Lately, I had had only an indistinct connection to my physical self; so I had to relearn all the basics, rewire the connections.

Like sleeping, for example. Hang around a cat and you notice how much they sleep. A lot. I've heard it said that two-thirds of a cat's life is spent asleep.

All my life I have fought sleep. If I was tired in the morning or during the day, I drank a lot of coffee. When I was tired at night, I sank in front of the television and went into a semiconscious dullness for a few hours instead of hitting the sack immediately. Next day, I was still tired.

This weariness built up. I called it my *sleep deficit*. I couldn't balance it with a few "early nights." I had years of losses of sleep time to bring into the black.

Alice and I began to have cat naps together. This was easy to do. If I was ensconced on the couch in front of the TV, she usually got on my lap and slept. Instead of continuing to watch the program, I would switch off the set and doze with her, perhaps only for five or ten minutes.

The effect was immediate and salutary. I awoke less frazzled, calmer; the world seemed manageable. Small things—a jar lid not turning easily, a ringing phone, my fumbling fingers on a shoelace—did not irritate me as they had.

These short sleeps cleared my mind. They made room for new information. In my tired, semiconscious state I had been more likely to be half-dreaming, living in my subconscious rather than in the room. The more awake I was, the less formidable the world seemed. And the room.

When Alice awoke from these naps, she stretched. It was a real workout. First, her back rose up in an upside-down *U*—as if an invisible string were pulling her from the ceiling—with all her legs stretched down to spindly toes. Then her front legs went forward, her back end up. Finally, she thrust head and shoulders forward and up, back end down, rear legs stretched out behind to their full length. Her spine was like an elastic.

When I stood up from crouching over my desk or keyboard, I limped to wherever I was going in a continuing Quasimodo posture. My backbone was becoming compressed and weak; I had the beginnings of a stoop.

I saw how Alice gave her backbone a lot of attention. Keeping it limber made sense. After all, it was the centre of her nerve endings, the communications network to her senses and limbs. So it was important to keep the channels open.

Because my backbone was in bad shape, I was not receiving the messages clearly; movement had become more difficult. And the more trouble I had moving, the less I wanted to move.

I started working on my back. Every day I lay down on a carpet and pressed my spine against the floor. There I flexed and undulated it, gradually freeing it up. It turned out to be the key to unlocking the rest of my body.

Muscles stiff from disuse began to wake up and clamour for attention. Eventually I started doing calisthenics, trying to make my body supple and agile—a cat's body. But even if I had no time or inclination for any other exercise, I made sure that I spent a few minutes on the floor each day, flexing and stretching that old spine of mine. For this little bit of attention also seemed to wake my mind up. When I got up from the floor, the world around me had a new clarity.

🐾 🐾 🐾

After a stretch, Alice usually headed outdoors. She spent most of her wakeful one-third out there. To me, going outside was distressing. Lately I had been avoiding leaving the house as much as possible. When Alice came to get me at my desk, I would let her out the door and close it behind her. She would stare back over her shoulder at me for a moment, give what looked to me like a shrug and a sigh, and then amble down the path. But in Cat School, I followed her out.

We would wander around the garden, from tree to bush to shrub to grassblade, checking, I suppose, for cat messages. Alice might find a spot, perhaps under the cedar trees, and settle down, not sleeping, just sitting. I crouched beside her and waited. The time went by. Little air currents blew her fur and rustled the branches. Smells would come up from the soil and tree roots, and small noises became apparent that would jerk Alice's head in their direction. Everything was happening now.

The sky surrounded us. Looking into it, away from the strictures of laid out yards and streets and the squareness of the houses, was a blessed peek at an infinity where the blueness or greyness vanished into a pure haze. There were no sign posts. It was free fall up there. And down here, everything stretched out. Time was on the clock inside the house. This was one of Alice's spots.

Alice had a few choice spots where she went and sat. Sometimes she would sleep in them, but mostly she sat and looked. I thought of them as places of contemplation. There were times when she did not want me there with her. If I approached, she would "humph" and move off. It was like disturbing a Buddhist monk at practice or an ecstatic Kabbalist in *kavannah*, reciting the Name.

For I was convinced that Alice was doing a sort of cat meditation in these places; she was appreciating a state of being. And I found out that she needed them each day as much as food. At all costs she would try to get to them. In fact, one of them almost cost her her life. And Mary's.

12

Alice and the Rock

For some time I had coveted Alice's places of contemplation. I wanted my own spot, a respite from the city where I had been living for over twenty years.

When my parents were alive, there was the option of visiting them for awhile in the small town where I had grown up. The visits gave me a "time-out" from the hectic atmosphere, noise, and bad air of what was for me essentially an alien environment. So after reaching a settlement in the lawsuit, I used my recovered royalties to make a down payment on a cottage close to that same small town. (Like a cat, I liked familiar places.)

The cottage was on a river, therefore cheaper; most people wanted to be beside a lake. After staying at the place for awhile, I realized why.

A lake is calm stability, the water contained, giving the impression of a controllable, unchangeable life. But a river, always moving, reminds one of life rushing past, changing as you watch it, passing you before you've grasped it.

The river, like the nagging question of life, would not stop, could not be pinned down. What I had chosen as my place of repose was sticking the question in my face. I could not escape it. For the first few years, I found that I could rarely look at that river.

It was a fast river. The cottage was built on a billion-year-old rock, the Precambrian Shield at its southernmost edge, and the water had worn its way through this rock. In the winter, the river was a torrent, never freezing over at our shoreline, but driven to a frenzy by bottlenecks of ice to the north and south of us. Deep, black, and cold, replenished by heavy snowfalls, it raced past the Big Rock like herds of wildebeest, a thunder of high, rushing water.

Alice loved that rock. It had a crevice at the top into which she would disappear and emerge down below on a ledge of granite that jutted out over the water. There, on summer mornings, she lay in the cool western exposure and surprised passing canoeists with the sight of a cat on an apparently inaccessible platform. She looked like a lynx in its lair. This was Alice's favourite spot.

The first winter that we stayed there, the river was at its most violent. The air was so cold that a thin layer of ice had formed at the edge of our shoreline, making a deceptive walkway about two feet wide. We had just arrived and were busy unpacking when Mary noticed that Alice wasn't around.

She went outside to call her, and saw that there were paw prints leading down the steep snowbank to the place at the river's edge where we swam in the summer. These prints went out onto that sliver of ice alongside the swirling river and disappeared from Mary's view.

Scrambling down the slope, over the edge where the concrete steps ended and where the wooden steps, dismantled for the season, usually began, Mary reached the swimming area. There, out on the ice sidewalk, was Alice. Snow had blocked the entrance to the crevice at the top of the Big Rock, and now the only way to get to her ledge, her beloved spot, was a leap across several feet of roiling water, from a launching pad of wafer-thin ice.

Mary called frantically to her. The swollen river was moving so fast that she had to shout to be heard over the noise of it. Alice glanced back with a calm, bemused look and then moved a little further away along the ice. She was heading for the ledge.

Wary of stepping through, Mary got down on her stomach on that fringe of ice and started to push herself towards Alice. Her head was inches above the black freezing river. Cold spray covered her face and froze in her hair.

Alice was staring at the ledge now and she began to get that look that cats have when they're measuring a jump. It's an attitude of concentrated head, the calculations firing off, memories of other leaps recalled, small crouchings and extendings of the body, switchings of the tail, and widening and narrowing eyes.

And just as Alice had completed her geometry, just as her beloved ledge had formed an X at the end of the arc of a dotted line in the jumping program of her brain, Mary grabbed her leg.

Kicking, squirming, hissing—no different a cat than when she had been saved from the alley that first day, Alice was dragged off the ice and carried up to the cottage.

Not that this stopped her. From then on we had to keep an eye on her in the winter, sometimes forming a defensive line in front of the Big Rock, like a flag football game, as Alice dodged and feinted her way towards the edge.

She was always going for the edge. Cat School was no day in the country.

13

Alice and the Snake

A lice took easily to life at the cottage, rummaging through the woods, racing over the rocks, making midnight forays into the utter blackness and stillness that surrounded us. Even our other cat, Chico, the quintessential urbanite, who always looked as if he were wearing a sharkskin suit and thin, expensive Italian shoes, was soon nosing around the forest.

I watched them with envy. I had never been a woodsman. Furthermore, my years in the city had made me a stranger to this silent landscape without streetlights or a corner store. Here there was no familiar blanket of human culture to smother the naked mystery of existence. This was their world and I was out of my element.

Alice adapted immediately. She did not have to reach far inside to tap her ancient ways. Take the snake, for instance.

The very first time Alice saw a snake, she took up the Snake Position. I knew it right away from having seen all those TV nature programs and animal adventure movies where the mountain lion or Lassie rears her head back and draws one arm behind the ear and up, with the paw aimed down, so that the S-shape, the question mark, the swan's neck of arm and paw looks exactly like a snake about to strike.

So it was obvious, out there in the dry grass around the Big Rock, in the growing heat of 11:30 on a July morning, that a snake had come around to the cool side of the cottage and Alice was pointing it out in ancestral fashion.

I was impressed and astounded that this city cat, this girl of the urban alleyways, knew what to do out here on the Precambrian Shield. Meet a snake, assume the Snake Position. It was a tableau, that formation of cat and snake, a scene from Animal Live Theatre, a primeval ritual utterly independent of my observation, as I stood thick in my shorts and beach thongs, all squint and stomach. These were the ways of the earth.

Alice's face was set and determined, without fear or hatred, full of innocent concentration like a baby holding a pencil. She did not hiss or growl. She did not move. She simply held her stance, paw up and curved. The air was hot, still and dry, full of insect sounds and the moving river. My head was stuffed; my eyes hurt; my cotton wool suit snug over my senses. I had no idea where I was or when.

46

In fact, we were in the Garden and Alice was saying: *"Hey, the snake's here!"*

I crept over slowly and saw that the snake was much larger than what I imagined living around us. It had beautiful neon skin and it seemed calm and thoughtful. Here was another animal, one of us, and it was out in the day. I picked up Alice and took her away from it, for all our sakes.

At the cottage, Alice opened up the world of animals to me. I was one of them, and we lived together in this landscape, the terrain where humans had their proper place—not lords and masters but merely part of the scheme of things.

And she unlocked the cultures of rocks and trees and insects. Here they all were, carrying on their lives whether human beings were present or not. If a tree fell in this forest, it would indeed make a sound: a squirrel or a blue jay or an otter would hear it. No humans were necessary to actualize an event.

There was something going on, with me or without me, that I could sense but could not put words to.

14

Alice and the Bug

Taking up the Snake Position was indicative of the way Alice communicated with me—without spoken language but with signs and symbols. For me, this was a relief. Lately I had had little to say to people. My heart was full of what others really did not want to hear about and I couldn't blame them. I felt shy and ashamed and had begun even to stammer now and then. It was hard for me to make small talk. In any case, there was not much happening in my life that related to what other people were doing. I didn't know anyone else who was following a cat around.

Alice had no use for small talk. She dealt in large concepts and basics: sky, food, friendship. She understood how to cut through language, to get past its dangerous ability to isolate us from each other. She could use a simple action that contained incredible nuance and underlying purpose. Like the bug, for example.

One summer day, Mary and I were having a terrible argument. Shouting, slandering, recriminations, and hatred, the words escalated in harshness and trapped us in their echoes. There was no way out and no end in sight.

Alice had been sitting near us but left when the noise and venom became too much. Now there was a muffled cry from the cat door. I turned my head at the sound and saw Alice coming through with something in her mouth. She walked over to us and very carefully put it on the floor at our feet.

It was a bug, of such varied colours I had never seen in my life. It was totally unharmed, hardly wet from saliva. It moved around on the carpet and the sunlight glanced off its back, a beautiful mosaic. The argument stopped dead.

I don't know where Alice found that bug; I never saw its like again. And I don't know how she managed to carry it in her mouth without killing it. But she brought a wondrous thing to us, a reminder of the world beyond our petty and destructive fighting. She woke us from the madness, the waste of time and life we were perpetrating. We were distracted long enough so that the spell of hateful language was broken. Alice wanted to pull us out of it and she did so in the only way she could: she brought us a bug.

15

The Big Blue Car

Alice taught me a great deal about the pitfalls and limitations of spoken language. We spent our days in relative silence, but I never felt that we were not in continual communication. She was always immediately responsive; there was no warming-up necessary to our encounters. Our minds were rubbing up against each other as tangibly as her body was winding around my legs when we stood in the garden together. We stood looking and listening and the world would become the apex of an invisible triangle that joined it to Alice to me to it. I trusted her. She was true. There was no need for words. She reminded me of what I had not thought about for a long time, of when I was taking care of my father, many years before.

In 1979, my Dad had been diagnosed with Alzheimer's disease and could not be left by himself. That summer, my mother went into hospital for five weeks and it fell to me to look after him. Although I was in the midst of running my own band, I had to leave it all behind and the group soon broke up.

My father and I would drive back and forth between visiting my mother in hospital in Toronto and staying in the little town where my parents lived, ninety miles north. Dad owned a huge, dark blue, '75 V-8 Chrysler, a Newport, a real gas-guzzler. He had loved to drive that car. But in the previous spring, a doctor caused his license to be revoked, so I had to take the wheel now. He didn't seem to mind that. After all, he was the one who had taught me how to drive.

At night, returning north from the hospital, the powerful car slipped us through the summer darkness like a ship. The highway would be almost deserted. We rolled down the windows so the warm air rushed in, bringing smells from the fields that spread away on either side of us and vanished into black silence.

Inside, it was also silent. For my father had become embarrassed by his lapses of memory and hardly spoke, afraid that he might be asking the same question he had asked seconds before. And I was quiet as well; also embarrassed, and worse (to my everlasting shame and regret), impatient with him, impatient with the collapse of what had been his humorous, curious, intelligent mind. And more: self-absorbed, lost in panic, knowing that my band and my career were falling apart back in the city. So talking was difficult for both of us.

But we had always loved being on the road. When I

was young, he used to take me on car trips in the springtime, down south to America. We stayed in old motels by the side of the highway where the whoosh of the transports could be heard all night. Mornings, we started out early, rising before dawn and travelling the empty two-lane blacktops while the dew was still wet on the windshield.

We knew that about each other: we loved to drive. And now we loved the feel of this big blue car tearing through the night. We listened to the tires whistling over the highway and we did not speak. We just drove.

And as the weeks went by up and down that road, as the days were spent getting him up and dressed and preparing his meals, and hours sitting on the porch— sitting with nothing but the sound of the trees between us, and hope like a distant bird in the white blue sky— I found that we also loved each other; and in a way I had not experienced before. I realized that I loved him now not as my father but as a fellow creature, a fellow animal hanging on to life, wrestling with its impenetrable scheme and skewed sense of justice.

Language could no longer disguise these bare facts: that each of us simply endured time and filled space and we shared them together. Of more than this we could not speak. For what could I say to my Dad that would have given him anything to look forward to other than a few more hours of us sitting together or a few more miles on the road? Luck had run out for good. I would not lie to him.

So we left our roles as father and son. We became two living beings entangled in the mystery of living. Bonded by this shared fate, the bizarre condition of finding ourselves breathing in a deaf universe, so apparent now in our silence, we developed a sympathy for each other and then a trust and then finally an agreement unspoken: that neither of us would cause pain to the other.

It was the most and the least that anyone can do. We had no loftier ambitions. When the hours became unbearable, we climbed into the Chrysler and cruised the back roads outside town, clouds of dust billowing out from under the wheels behind us.

Nothing was said. We only sat and looked out as the machine hurtled us through time and space. The world flashed by; inside was immutable. When he died that winter, I lost a friend.

The big blue car still sits in front of the cottage, rusting out, its huge V-8 quiet now. Squirrels climb through holes in the doors and store nuts in the upholstery. One season, a family of moles lived in the backseat. And every so often, a man with a tow truck will show up at the door and offer to haul it away for scrap. But I decline. The mass of silent dark metal is a reminder to me of those summer nights, and when I lean on it I can still hear the highway singing a song to my father.

16

Cat Talking

In Cat School, we used the cat's way of talking: with few words but plenty of body language. Alice also liked rituals. She even taught one of her own to Chico. This was the ceremony for letting me know that it was time to eat. Now when I came unsuspectingly into the kitchen, there would be two cats sitting in the centre of the floor, erect, with their backs to me, saying, "*Where's the grub?*"

Rituals worked to reaffirm our connection to each other. Whenever I opened the back door to let Alice out, she always waited a moment while I ran my hand down her back, from the top of her head to the tip of her tail. It is hard to say how we started this habit. In my mind, it was as if I were imparting a magic charm to her, a shield of protection that would keep her from harm and secure her safe return home to me, back from the dangers of the world she was entering. It was like a laying on of hands, warding off the evil spirits from a warrior on a perilous quest.

It sounds crazy but I was crazy for her, for my friend, and I could not control a wild world that lay outside our door. This physical action, rubbing a cat's fur, was my feeble human's attempt to keep away the demons and to give Alice one last reminder that here was her home and not to forget to come back. Come back over the fence and make our lives happy.

What it meant to Alice I'll never know. But she always waited for my hand; it was a last contact before we left each other for awhile, and that caress became one more link in the chain that bound us together.

We also had the Ritual of Staring. This is a very complicated mode cats have of re-establishing contact. They do not take events for granted. If you come into a room, they're liable to look up at you with a stare of alarming intensity, as if they've never seen you before. "It's me, Alice!" I found myself crying out at her wide-eyed, startled gaze. It made no difference. We would have to go through an etiquette.

First she squinted her eyes at me and I would squint back. This was an expression of mutual trust: we could close our eyes on each other; neither would attack while our guards were down. The squinting continued for a few moments and then changed rhythm, to a slow opening and closing of our lids. Here we acknowledged our mutual presence in the room, in the universe, as friends. It was like blowing a kiss.

Then, politely, we directed our gaze slightly to one side, not to impinge on the other's modesty; and then back again for more squinting as our eyes met. Back and forth our eyes would go until at last we closed them altogether and relaxed and sank into the luxury of being two separate living things at peace with each other, mingling our separate times on the earth and occupying the same place in friendship. And now the rug that we lay on was no longer an object that had been purchased to cover a floor. Now it was a collection of molecules like us, and together we were all swirling through the universe.

After a while, Alice would yawn and stretch and go get a drink. This was the work of a lifetime.

However, sometimes I spoke words to Alice and she understood whatever I said to her as if the words had formed a hologram in the air between us, an invisible, graphic representation of what I was saying. She always responded to my meaning, no matter what language it was in. I spoke to her now and then in Yiddish which she seemed to enjoy hearing. Usually the words were terms of endearment such as I used to hear at home. But often I would speak whole paragraphs to her, and the effect was always to relax her. It made her purr and close her eyes as if she were listening to some old, half-forgotten song.

And purring was a language that Alice spoke to me. When she sat on my lap and let me know that life was good and we were pals, the engine in her throat and chest would sing like a pump house. I didn't have to guess if she were having a good time; Alice broadcast her enjoyment of the situation. But her purring was not confined to communicating with me.

She purred sometimes just sitting in the sun; I would come upon her like that. This is how I realized that cats appreciate the world when they are in it. Their actions were not only those of defence and survival. Part of Alice's time was spent simply enjoying being alive. Her purring was a kind of prayer being sent out into the universe, a joyful song praising the wonder of living.

From watching Alice, I began to understand a little of what the Kabbalah meant by *Creation*. It was not only a place and the concept of that place; it was also the experience in that place. It was a way of being, *the* way. "Creation" was the experience of being, of living totally in the immediacy of the moment (*time*) and the spot (*space*) where you were. That was what Alice did for those moments in her spots of contemplation. She was experiencing Creation with all her energies.

What did it feel like? I sat with her and imagined but I only met my mind there. Creation had to be wider than the inside of my own head. It must be the reality of the whole of life that I still was so very far away from.

17

The Gantse Megillah

It was the whole of life that Alice showed me as I lived beside her. The *Gantse Megillah* as it is called in Yiddish: the whole story.

In the span of a cat's days, one gets to see a complete lifetime: how one comes into it, knowing so little, learning to get around; and then making the choices of how to spend the duration of it—what one makes of life. The cats give us a perspective on how contained and temporary is this situation. Look, they say, here it is. Beginning to end. Same as yours. What happens in between?

What happens in between the garages in that narrow passageway as you run frantically back and forth? This is your life. What will you do with it?

Alice, living her life beside me, tried to show me what to do with it. In her Cat School, her lesson was simple: in her plain physical language, in a symbolism of ritual and habit, she tried to wake me up and open the door. And go out.

So the life went by. Alice woke me in the mornings and dragged me to the door in the days and lay beside me in the nights; always keeping me aware of her presence, pulling me out of my thoughts; engaging my attention and not letting me slide.

When she came into the house from her rounds outdoors, she always let out a "yip," almost a bark, and I would answer her. Then she raced into the room where I was, in a great flurry of energy, as if this moment, the one we were in, were the most exciting moment that ever was.

And there were times when Mary had gone out, and I was upstairs, that Alice would think she was alone in the house. She set up the most heartrending wailing until I shouted out her name. Then she would bound up the stairs, peek around the door, and now there was nothing more wonderful in the universe than that we were here together in this place.

Some nights she climbed up on my chest as I lay in bed, and stretched out her body with her face only inches from mine. She would stare into my eyes with her own huge, almond-shaped ones, so intently that I was almost frightened. *What do you want, Alice?* She would just keep looking, until I came out of myself, came to her, here in the room, and really saw her there, another creature in the world, and here we were.

So I watched Alice. She presented to me the vision of her elegant movements as she turned and swayed among the trees and grasses. She gave me the example of the strength of her mind as she willed her way to the places that her spirit required.

And she tried to take me with her. There were mornings when she got me out of bed to show me a particularly brilliant sunrise; nights at the cottage when she summoned me from my chair to follow her to the deck, there to encounter the river bathed in silver moonlight. She would settle down beside me as if, by example, I too might settle down and see, see what was all around me, the life of it.

Intermittently I practised what Alice tried to teach me. I had an idea of where I wanted to go; there were glimpses of the place I now knew of as Creation. But these momentary gleams of light were surrounded by days and weeks of dismal confusion and dark moods.

I began to fret about what I was doing with my life. My career was at a complete standstill. I became tired of this atmosphere of being in limbo. I initiated various recording projects, attempting to get myself back into the human world. But they all came to nothing and, in the process, Cat School was abandoned.

The time wasted away while I remained locked in my isolation, ignoring weather and light and even Alice. And then Alice got sick.

18
Sickness

In the seventh year of her life, Alice began drinking a lot of water. A blood test revealed that her kidneys were damaged and failing. Our vet, Jack, told us that it was a condition that could have begun from her very first days in the alley. There, starved and parched, she may have licked up some radiator fluid antifreeze which tastes sweet to an animal, but is so deadly that it immediately and irremediably impairs the kidneys.

We put her on a low-protein diet and sprinkled powdered vitamins on her food. We gave her homeopathic remedies from an eyedropper. It seemed to be working.

That summer at the cottage, she bounced back. After a winter and spring of depleted energy, she was her old self among the trees and on the Big Rock. I felt we were blessed with a second chance and that this had only been a wake-up call.

Then, on the morning we were leaving to return to the city, Alice came to get me and I followed her out to the north side of the cottage. She seemed agitated and I couldn't figure out what she wanted. She stood looking up at me as I gazed around. Finally I noticed.

A tree had fallen against the roof during the night, a tree that had not appeared diseased or weak. Neither Mary nor I had heard it fall. Alice had come to warn me that things were not quite right.

And they weren't. Back in the city that autumn, Alice's health deteriorated again. X-rays showed that her kidneys had swollen up. She could no longer drink enough water and became dehydrated. Her body needed help and we began to give her infusions of fluid with a needle in the soft folds of fur on the back of her neck.

It was a hard thing to do to a friend. But I thought if we kept her alive long enough, she might recover her equilibrium and get her strength back. Perhaps the swelling of her kidneys could come down.

There was discussion of a kidney transplant, a very new procedure. But I knew that Alice would not want her life to become that of hospitals and medicines. The surgery had a very small chance of success and she would have been miserable.

So we tried what we could. We hoped and we lived in dread. I knew the feeling well and I began to sink back behind the Wall. But Alice would not let me go there.

19

The Deck

That winter, when she was very sick, she would lie at the top of the stairs in the hall. I was afraid that the drafts along the floor might sap her warmth and energy. I set up a chair beside her and took her on my lap. She would fall into a deep sleep and afterwards seem stronger and in better humour.

Then, in December, there was a week of unusually warm days. We left the door to the deck open so Alice could go out there and sit in the sun. But it was still winter and the temperatures were relatively low. Again I feared her getting cold and I put one of the plastic patio chairs out on the deck.

Dressed in my winter coat with a comforter wrapped all around it, I sat in the chair and placed Alice in my lap. Here she seemed to descend into the deepest and heaviest of sleeps. They went on for literally hours. And on waking, Alice was refreshed and more her old self.

These sleeps were obviously of crucial importance. The problem for me was sitting still for so long. If I moved an arm or adjusted a leg, she would wake up and jump off. Yet the longer her sleeps were uninterrupted, the healthier she would be after them.

To stave off pains in my limbs and the urge to go to the bathroom, I tried to think of other things. Given my state of mind, these thoughts turned inevitably to bad thoughts: wrongs, thwarted career, endlessly re-hashed arguments—the tired old newsreels of the human mind, showtimes daily in the Theatre of the Self. And when I became agitated by these thoughts, as I inevitably did, Alice would wake up and leave.

I tried to think of something else but it all eventually found its way back into the old Theatre. So I realized that I had to stop thinking. But what would I think about when I wasn't thinking?

At first, the most I could do was to try and shut down a thought as it began. My mind would generally career down a track at full speed, totally out of control, until I could pull the keys from out of the ignition. Simply stop it dead.

Or, to mix the metaphors, I was like a combination batter-pitcher catching my own line drives to centre field.

After a while, the mind gets confused and puzzled at being foiled all the time. It doesn't quite shut off but sort of sits there humming. It's as if you've reached a different operation of the program. Now it is awaiting further commands. This is where its normal usage stops. You're on your own from here. Where do you want to go? And suddenly, I went out.

I went out, from inside my mind, onto the deck, into the sun, with Alice on my lap, and a real tree opposite me, with a real bird in it. I was here.

It was huge. A great expanse of energy without duration or boundaries. Nothing was unfamiliar but everything was constantly new, bursting with living.

I felt no ambition. I had no desire. I just was. Like the present tense of the verb "to be" that does not exist in Hebrew: you can't say it. You can only *be* it.

It was what the Kabbalah had been talking about. I was in Creation. I was a living, breathing creature knowing nothing else but living and breathing, doing nothing else but being.

And by only being, not doing or thinking or judging, I became aware, in a way that was not conscious of my awareness, of the world in its simple fact of existing, without explanation or apparent purpose.

This was the true situation, the one we called life, and it had no explanation.

I felt no fear of this lack of explanation, this mystery. It had become a given. My mind was filled only with the awesomeness of this place I was in. I felt release from all my concerns, emptied of everything but the "physical-ness" of Creation. I felt comfortable here; I was where I was meant to be. It felt like Home.

Guilt left my heart. Finally I was doing what I was meant to do. I had been created with the ability to receive that which was created to be received. I was the missing piece of a jigsaw puzzle, a receptor that completed the picture of the world. And I felt gratitude for being able to witness this picture.

I was doing my job, the job of all living creatures: I was appreciating Creation. I was connecting time and space. I was in the Right Place at the Right Time. I was alive. I was nowhere. I was now here.

I realized the obvious: that Creation goes on all the time despite me while I'm in my private theatre. And that what I had just experienced was the real thing and the rest was a smoke screen and a mirror.

I had punctured my bubble to be with Alice. I had walked through the Wall to here, where she was all the time. I had realized that I was living. Just in time. I was forty-six years old and my cat had just saved my life.

20

Culture and Creation

W hat life had Alice saved? It was here, now, the life taking place in the moment I was in whether I was aware of it or not. It was the life I was wasting, the gift of time I was frittering away, ignoring the wondrous experience of this place, Creation. I was merely existing here, benumbed to it by that overwhelming tumult: the human story, the story our minds tell us.

In the human story, the universe revolves around us and we are the tragic and glorious heroes. Our minds are so filled with the constant chattering of the telling of this tale, and our attention is so focused on the events of its twisting plot, that we do not notice where we are. Womb to grave, it is mostly what we experience as Life.

I could not stay in Creation. As soon as I left the deck that afternoon, my mind took over and began the story again. Remaining aware of the life that Alice had saved was a problem. For the story not only kept me out of

Creation; it stopped me from remembering that Creation was there. Or rather, here. I was *there*, out in that story. It seemed there were only two ways about it: I was either in Creation or out. When I was "out of it," the human story would become my only experience of existence; Creation was not an option.

The story was so omnipresent, so indivisible from who I was, that I could not recognize when it was operating and controlling me. It was imperative that I find a way to identify it, like a disease, so I could separate myself from it. It needed to be objectified, put out *there*, away from me, back inside Creation where it belonged.

It was Alice who gave me a perspective on the human story. She had shown me that it was not the only one. In Cat School, I saw that Alice had her own way of looking at everything, of operating in and interpreting the world. This was her culture, and it was different than mine. But my human culture, though composed of many national and ethnic ones, seemed monolithic in comparison to Alice's, or the snake's, or the Big Rock's. In the manner in which it enveloped my perceptions, it worked not as *a* culture, but as *the* culture.

Every minute of my waking life had been spent in its environment. It defined me before I knew that I was being defined. This was "culture" not as music, art, dance, etc., but the total range of activities, ideas and peculiarities of the human species: clocks, computers, concrete; work, war, wardrobe; the opposable thumb, the upright stance, the endless talking; the pandemic presence of all things human; the products and styles consequent from being this kind of animal.

So I called it *Culture*. Capitalized, self-convinced it is the supreme operating system for life, it is the ultimate advertising campaign that promotes one thing only: HUMAN. Buy it. Swallow it. Live it. *Culture* was so pervasive that I did not realize that I was just a participant in a system: I thought it was life itself.

Culture is the human neighbourhood. It fosters the mindset that keeps the particularly human interpretation of the world constantly at the forefront of our perceptions. For most of our lives, we behave as if the concerns and activities of our human street are all that exist. Intellectually, we may know better; practically, we rarely venture out of our perceptual suburbia.

But take a walk out of that neighbourhood and other ways of structure and conduct are suggested. That is what Cat School had done. The time with Alice had taught me that my way of seeing was merely a product of the human point of view, our adaptation to reality.

For it was reality that *Culture* wrestled with: the stark facts of being alive, knowing death, and having no explanation for either. To the human mind, this mystery is a horror, and *Culture* works to stifle the fear of that horror. It is the ersatz explanation for carrying on. It is our attempt to give our lives purpose. It works but it works too well. *Culture* keeps us from realizing that we are alive. It keeps us out of Creation.

Now I could see that Alice's culture had integrated her life seamlessly into Creation. She found her spots and moments where she could appreciate it. But I was living like a moth in an opaque jar beside a candle. Creation was out there, shining on brightly, while I flew around in circles, beating my brains out against the hard surface of *Culture*, unaware that the jar had no lid.

I was always in Creation. Creation is where we all are. It is where "living" takes place. It is the Place we human beings measure, in atoms and miles and light years, through microscopes and from the tops of mountains and off the antennae of satellites, but of which we do not know the ultimate dimensions and perhaps physically never will.

In fact, it has only two dimensions: space, apparently limitless, of No End; and time, which we also measure, in hours and aeons and in the boundaries of our limited lives. Time from a beginning upon which we speculate, to an end we can only argue about, is also probably of No End: *Ayn Sof.*

That's all there is. Why there is "space," why there is "time," why life had to be made in these formats, we do not know. But here we are and it is strange.

We ourselves are strange. We try to disguise that fact even as we cannot stop peeking at it. But the truly strange is what we hide from.

And that is: the truth of the spot and the moment you are in: the acknowledgement of the period at the end of this sentence. And the paper you are touching that it is printed on, and the time that is going by as you get to the next one.

Time is all we have. Most of it is stolen from us. And mostly we want it to be stolen from us, for we are scared of time. In *Culture,* "Time is money"; we "buy time" and we "spend" it. It is "on our hands" to be rid of, "wasted." Seen as a commodity, time seems controllable (*we can get more!*) and we barter our lives with it.

I began to feel that in Creation time was an ether, an atmosphere. It surrounded me as a river its inhabitants. Time had molecules and I moved through it as if it were air. And I could pollute it. Most of my days had a hole in their ozone layer from the exhaust fumes of this constantly idling engine of my mind.

The days are all we have. Day-by-day the time goes and we alone are responsible for our own. How many can we let go by without ever having truly known that we are alive? That we are in a strange place and that it is of awesome wonder?

When I stepped out of *Culture,* and allowed myself to realize without thinking, I encountered the true purpose of my existence: to experience Creation. Not to judge it or measure it but to be in it, appreciate it.

We were created to be in awe. Our minds were made to receive beauty. We are the receptacle for the electrical plug of reality; the radio receiver for the broadcast of the giant program of the universe. Any time spent not receiving is not living. Any place inhabited away from Creation is not lived in.

In the days that followed, I went back to Cat School, to watching Alice and being with her. I bought a rug and placed it on my desk, over top of the papers and files, and drew back the curtains from windows that had been covered over for months. Alice lay on the rug in the sun, and I sat beside her, looking out the window at the light hitting the cars and houses in the street. And I would see them, as they were, light and reflection; and be there, in that place and that moment with Alice, practising what she had shown me. Whenever *Culture* threatened to engulf me, Alice alerted me to it; simply her presence here was enough to remind me that there was another way of looking at the world.

I will not pretend that I had become enlightened. I was able to "be" in Creation only occasionally. My mind's address was still the same pit. However, now I knew not only that there was somewhere else; now I had been there. I knew what I was missing and, with Alice beside me, I felt that I would always be able to reach it.

And when I had discovered what I had been missing, just as I reached the place where Alice had beckoned me to come, where she always was, and where, because she was there, I felt safe to be, just as I got there, she left. Just like a cat.

21

The Chapter You Can Skip

This is the chapter you can skip. I say that to warn a
close friend who hates to read about the death of
an animal and this is where an animal dies.

I had to include it because it is the truth of what happened and I have tried to tell the truth in this story.

This is Alice's story and I will tell how she died. It is for
Alice's sake. Alice did not shirk from her death and
neither will I.

Her death was as important to me as the death of anyone I have ever loved. It was the death of a great soul.

This is what happened:

On the last night of her life, when she no longer had the strength to climb up on my bed (I realize that fact only at this moment), Alice went into my cupboard and lay down among some clothes that had fallen and some boxes of shoes, with her back to me.

From my position, my head on the pillow, I could just see her ears. I thought in my craziness and misery that if I could only watch her ears all night, she would stay there and be safe. She would live.

But my will failed me, like so many times before, and when I awoke some time later, she had left. From then on, she was out of my hands, gone to dying.

The next morning, we gathered in the upstairs front room: Alice and Mary and I and our other cat, Chico. Alice was lying on her stomach with her paws in front and we sat in a semi-circle around her. She was squinting at us in the cat sign of friendship. Her fur was dull and matted and she seemed to come back and forth from somewhere far away.

Mary left for work and Chico wandered off and I remained, lying on the carpet and reading a book while Alice continued to sit, her eyes closed, her body swaying a little.

Suddenly, she got up with violence, like something had grabbed her and pulled her up. She went towards the door but her legs gave out and she collapsed to the carpet. I rushed over and tried to hold her up. But she shook me off, tore free from me and, as if something were forcing her, as if it had her in its grasp, she began to move down the hall.

She was stumbling from side to side, banging her body into the wall on her left and then the bannister on her right, like she was being flung against them. There was an overwhelming sense of another presence surrounding us. She was being dragged by something to somewhere and we were all alone against it in an empty place. I stood there, frozen. Everything seemed to be made of white light.

And suddenly it felt that the day had split open: it was no longer a day. There was no more time in the universe but a force that had broken all structure and was carrying my friend to her death.

She staggered and weaved her way to the end of the hall. She went into the bathroom and lay down behind the toilet. I tried to pick her up, to take her out of there, but she gave out such a cry of agony that I had to let her go. I sat down beside her on a small bench and waited for Mary to come home for lunch.

I began to talk to God about my friend, to plead her case, and now there were three of us in the universe against this thing and none of us could control it.

Mary came home and lifted Alice from behind the toilet. Alice cried out again so Mary carried her only as far as the bathtub where she laid her down.

Mary had to return to work and I sat beside Alice and now I talked only to her. I told her how she had helped me and I thanked her and I asked her to forgive me for not having been the friend she deserved but that she had been the best friend I had ever had. I told her how the world had been a better place for her having been in it; that she was better at being a person than I was and that I needed her to stay here because I was no good without her and the world was no good if she couldn't be in it and I loved her so much that she was taking my heart right out of me right now with her.

And then I tried to woo her back to me. I reminded her about the cottage and the rock and all the wonderful places of hers. And about sitting on the deck at night, the two of us, with the river moving down below. And I said that I would buy a truck and we would drive together all over the place. We would drive all over the world if only she would not leave me in this terrible place where my friend has to die.

I began to call all kinds of veterinarians, trying to get a remedy.

One time Alice lifted her face, and her eyebrows were drawn back and up, and her eyes were wide and staring at something with such fury and anger, like my father's face when he was dying.

Mary came home from work. We went out to buy some food. When we returned, Alice was dead.

They say animals want to die alone. Maybe she had waited all day for me to leave.

We had to bury her. It was winter and the ground was frozen. We boiled huge pots of water and poured them on the ground in the backyard. I started to dig a hole. We poured more boiling water into it. The wet earth stuck to the shovel and clouds of steam rose from the grave. It began to rain. A wind was blowing through the cedars, making them bend over. As I dug, I could hear Mary weeping, keening, through the upstairs window. The security light over the back door in the next yard was going on and off, on and off, crazily.

When I had finished digging, I came back in the house and saw that Mary had laid Alice on the couch and had wrapped her in a piece of white muslin. I carried her out and placed her in the grave. I turned back a corner of the muslin and saw her face for the last time. We put some cedar branches on her and covered her up with the wet earth. I recited the Shema.

We sat in the back room, looking out at the fresh grave, and drinking the fig brandy that my mother's Rabbi had given me. We sat up all night drinking, just trying to get the pain past those first few hours when it's like a razor that has cut you away from the one you love. The light rain spattered on the ground in the yard and that backdoor light continued to turn on and off like a strobe. Alice used to trigger that automatic light when she was coming home from the alley. That's how you knew she was safe.

On the morning after Alice's death, when Mary walked down Shannon Street on her way to work, all the cats in the neighbourhood lined the edge of the sidewalk, each in front of his or her house, sitting bolt upright as she passed by. Even Chico was there, who never ventured beyond the yards, looking bewildered at his own action, drawn by some unheard call. They all sat there, silent, staring straight ahead. I cannot begin to explain this.

I spent the day wandering the city. It was a warm day with brilliant sunshine. People were out in the day and Alice was no longer in the world.

22
Entry

Oct. 24/95, Big Rock.

It's a beautiful pink and blue sunrise, three hundred and sixty degrees around the sky. The clouds are moving rapidly and the leaves are being blown from the trees, fast, fast. I remember you so clearly this morning, Alice. I'm up early like you wanted me to be. It's a time of beautiful light—like you.

I remember you, in your self, your you-ness, Alice-ness, as real as if you were here somewhere, running around outside in the cold air, moving through the fallen leaves. It's an autumn sky: fast clouds of all shapes skimming by and the cool sun hitting the white tops of the western ones. The wind blows and it blows memories at me like the dead leaves into the river.

23

The Drop-Off

A cat will live alongside you and try to help you, teach you. And when they have taken you a certain distance, they drop you off.

Sometimes it may be because they are worn out, exhausted from the effort of trying to reach you. And sometimes because they have taken you as far as they can go with you. You have to find out how to make it on your own from there.

That might be the only way you will ever learn. You will sink or swim from that place midstream but the cat has already thrown you the lifeline. You have to see it and grab it.

In the last summer of Alice's life, she showed me her secret spots. I thought I knew all the particular places she went to, but one morning she got me out and took me on a tour around the cottage.

I saw a tree that she had been marking and special rocks where the moss had been worn away. She led me from one spot to the other and waited while I registered what was unique to each of them. Alice would scratch a bit at the tree or take up a position on a particular rock, sitting and looking around. We rested there together for awhile and then moved on to the next spot, maybe under some ferns where the ground was matted from use.

These were the secret places in her separate cat life; places I had not known about, where she disappeared to when she went out at dawn, and in the night when I called and looked for her and she came in out of nowhere.

Now she could never hide from me again. There were no more secrets between us; she had shown me all her cards. The game was over.

They were great spots, places where your soul could relax, and she passed them on.

24

Where Do We Go from Here?

Where do cats go when they die? Where does anybody go? I saw some clouds rushing across the sky and I thought that Alice was running away from me. Where are you running? What substance are you in now? Does such a clear personality, so loved by the living, just disappear into nothing? Or do each of your molecules contain who you are and so that quintessence of habits, likes and dislikes, memories and desires, is wafted into the universe. Why not a cloud?

Or the other. That the conglomeration of atoms that made you are all that you were. Together, they formed the brilliant machine and the place behind the eyes. But separated and scattered, no longer held together by the mysterious glue of life, you are no longer.

If we found the bits, painstakingly reconstructed them like after an airplane crash, could I get you back?

Otherwise, it seems like such a terrible waste for such a wonderful creature to have been formed, one who so loved Creation and with so much joy and who understood its purpose so much better than I, and then to have it disappear.

Sickness and disaster may be the consequences of physical nature, and death may be the corollary of life, but can there be no essence, no soul? And if there is a soul, where is Alice now?

And if there is someone who thinks that only humans have souls, shame on you. God laughs at your pride.

25

The Mourning After

For months after Alice died, I did not know what to do. It seemed impossible to have to be in the world without her. Her absence was like a weight holding me underwater. I wasn't sure how much longer I could keep my breath in, waiting for her to come back.

Creation was a far-off land, where Alice was, seemingly unreachable without her presence. Now I was in the familiar territory of grief. Here, all the dead waited for me and I did not want to face them.

I wanted back into normal life, away from the land of Death. All around me seethed the bustle and ambition of a modern city. People were out in it, looking for happiness. They too did not want to hear about the dying. *Culture* prodded and cajoled me to forget death and the dead together.

But I soon discovered that it was too late to go back. Once again, Death had ejected me from my day-to-day daydream by presenting the reality that *Culture* was trying to cover over—we know nothing. What I had been running from for all those years since my parents' deaths was shown to me now with the full force of the desolation and wretchedness I felt for the death of Alice: when we know in a visceral way that we really do know nothing, then we know too much; we are never able to go back into the world as it was.

But this time I had another place to go. Alice had shown me Creation. Here, there was more to life than the *Culture* that made me so aware of my misery. Here was a place where misery did not exist, nor ambition or the pursuit of happiness. Only *being* existed there and the peace that I had found from simply being. That was where Alice's presence was. If I wanted her presence, I had to find my way back to Creation and the only way to get there was past death.

Up to now, I had not dealt with death very well and I had to learn how. I had to face the reality of the world where Alice no longer was. For if I could not bear to be in a world where Alice did not exist, if I tried to escape back into a dream world of forgetting, of repressing the sorrow and the memories, then I would never be able to "be" at all.

In the other deaths in my life, my mourning had ended too soon. So I gave myself up to mourning Alice completely. I forced myself to feel every jab of the pain of missing her.

When someone we love dies, we begin to live in the land of Death. Its heavy atmosphere sits in a sadness and dread in the pit of the stomach and the centre of the chest. It is there when we go to sleep; and when we awake, as our consciousness surfaces, we remember that it waits for us, the long day of greyness.

The one we loved is gone. The moments of the day do not connect to anything. They reach out like severed nerves towards the presence of that one. Only having that presence here now could make the day bearable.

Ordinary tasks become onerous. Washing ourselves, dressing, going to work are all beside the point. There is only the death. Around us the world goes on as before. But we live in a new world now, a world without that one, and we have to get used to it.

We are not given much time to get used to it. Society seems to have placed an unstated, assumed expiry date on mourning. Perhaps a month or six weeks after a death, we are expected to be pretty much the same person we were before our loved one died. Whereas the truth is that we will never be that person again.

Anyone recovering from a broken leg is allowed more time to heal than those of us who have had a hole torn in our lives by the death of a loved one. We have been crippled by death and are disabled by grief. We must learn how to walk all over again. No one can predict or prescribe the length of time we will need.

✿ ✿ ✿

If it is hard enough taking a proper mourning period for a human death, it is almost impossible to be able to publicly grieve for the death of an animal. When an animal dies, we are not permitted to have the same feelings as when a human dies. We are expected to brush it off; it is not a serious event. The fact that we might have had as deep an attachment and as intense a relationship with the animal as with any human being does not matter. In our *Culture*, a human is deemed to be more important than an animal. Therefore the death of the animal is treated as inconsequential; and our lamenting for it, as an excessive indulgence. We are made to feel guilty and ashamed.

So it is difficult to grieve for an animal who was a friend, to reveal the extent of our sorrow. It is perhaps the loneliest of bereavements.

✿ ✿ ✿

It's alright to cry. It's alright to cry every day if we feel like it. It is as important as laughing. Because we are sad animals; and made sad with our longings. We may have these longings years after the one we love is gone. And then it's alright to cry when we long for them again. We kill ourselves if we stop it.

✿ ✿ ✿

When someone you love dies, you have to learn about it in every cell of your body. It takes a long time. All your separate personalities must adjust to the news of the death.

You have to experience the absence in every season of the year. I finally understood the custom among my people of the year-long mourning period, the *Yortzeit*.

Each change of weather brings different sensory memories of when you last lived through that season. The one who had been here the last time it snowed or when the leaves had fallen is gone; the one who sat with you when once the sun was hot is not here now in this warm July day. In every variation of atmosphere, I felt the sadness as intensely as the first day. They were all first days for my body.

The body misses the dead as much as the mind, more so perhaps. For the body has become addicted to the physical presence of the loved one. The sensory void after a death does sudden violence to its system. It has to "come off" the habit of having them around. If we do not give it the time to go through withdrawal, if we do not acknowledge the abrupt deprival of this physical dependency, then the body will rebel and sicken.

My body changed so I had to change; I had no choice. I recognized that I would never again be the person I was before Alice died. Whether that was good or bad was of no consequence. It was simply the truth that my life had been irremediably changed by the loss of her living presence. All the daily routines and habits carried on with that presence, taken for granted for years, all the daily sustenance given to me by our friendship, were absolutely and finally gone. Now I had to learn to live my life as a different person.

This was the "life" that Alice had saved. She made me open a door and I had to follow her out, into Creation. I could not throw away everything we had worked for. She had shown me something that I could never deny.

When I discovered that I could no longer return to my old world, I was able to go beyond my grief to look directly at that which stood between me and Alice: death itself.

26
The End

When I was a kid, no one told me that I was going to die. There were warnings about not running across the road or climbing in a tree because I could get killed. But I was left with the distinct impression that if I was very careful and followed all the rules, life would go on forever.

What would I have thought coming home from school one day and finding this note on my desk?

> *Dear Phil,*
>   *You have about seventy years.*
>   *Love,*
>   *Mom & Dad*
> *P.S. There's some chicken in the fridge.*

A note like that would have opened up a whole new perspective on things.

❦ ❦ ❦

One spring, I overheard my neighbour's son question-
ing his father about death. They were out in their garden, the man digging up some ground, getting ready to
plant. The boy was about six years old and his pet rabbit
had just died. He asked if people die. "Yes," his dad an-
swered. "Will Suzy die?" he inquired about his play-
mate. "Yes." "And will *you* die?" There was a slight
pause. "No," said his father.

❦ ❦ ❦

I once wrote a song called *I Don't Want To Die*. It went
like this:

> I *don't want to die.*
> *I* DON'T *want to die.*
> *I don't* WANT *to die.*
> *I don't want* TO *die.*
> *I don't want to* DIE.

Then a background choir came in singing:

> *"You got to* DIE*!"*

and the soloist would shout:

> *"No!"*

(It was not a hit song.)

❦ ❦ ❦

We humans like to think that we are the only ones suffering from an awareness of death. After living beside Alice, I began to suspect that it may not be so much that other animals do not know about death but rather that they do not dwell on it and they do not avoid it. They seem to assimilate it into their lives. And when it comes, they face it square on.

Humans don't want to admit that they will die. In *Culture*, we hide death and we hide from it. Here we live our lives in a dream of immortality where death is an embarrassment, as anyone knows who has received profferings of sympathy during a bereavement. You seem to have breached the bounds of good taste by having someone die on you. In fact, your sin is to have broken the illusion of *Culture* and so the living close their ranks.

We wrestle with death alone. The closest relatives and friends rarely speak to each other of the strangeness of having a mutual loved one disappear from the face of the earth. We may console each other in our sorrow but the really scary part is not discussed: what is death.

The simple reason for our reticence is that we have no answer. The more complicated one is that what we do know is so terrifying. We know that death is an unknowable. We know that we will all leave this world for an unknown place. We'd rather not talk about it.

There was no great separation between how Alice lived her life and how she met her death. She had found her spots to live in and she found her spot to die.

In her life, she spent her time in those spots, I believe, appreciating Creation, being there. Perhaps the spot where she went to her death was no different. She searched out a place to be alone, to be in Creation with all her concentration as death approached. In death, she was in Creation.

I saw that Alice had taught me not only about life, but also about death; not just how to live, but how to die. I only had to watch her.

My cat woke me up.

Over our years together, Alice had gradually brought me out of *Culture* and into Creation, out of my human dreaming and isolation into an awareness of the world as it was. It was a situation without explanation, a place where *we know nothing*, and I felt no fear there. On the contrary, I experienced an extraordinary state of peace of mind.

Death had also brought me out of *Culture* into an awareness that *we know nothing,* but here I was terrified— and for very good reason. For at the same moment that the unexplainable reality of life was made apparent to me and I lost my illusion of *Culture*, I also lost one of the main supports of my everyday life: the living relationship to someone I loved. I could not cope with such a complete explosion of structure. Simultaneously faced with the terror of death's mystery and power, and with the loss that it caused, I wept from fear and bewilderment as much as I did from grief. These separate effects

I had confused into one experience. The result was that I could not deal effectively with either.

Once I had dealt with the emotions of my grief, and could disentangle myself from that confusion, I was able to look directly at death and its mystery that so horrified me.

Then it became clear that the void which death had opened up in front of me, the place where we know nothing, that has no explanation, was no different from the place of unknowing that was Creation. They were both unfathomable mysteries.

In regions that I had segregated into one of horror and one where Alice spent her moments in her special spots, the result was basically the same. In both I was made completely aware that I was alive. In fact, what I was fearing about death was the consciousness of being.

For in becoming conscious of being, I also became conscious of non-being, of dying. This awareness had kept me isolated from living, from being in the world: I did not want to admit to the certainty of my own death.

At the time, that was all that consciousness had given me: the realization that some day I would no longer exist. To the human mind, born and bred in *Culture*, this is anathema. But consciousness turned out to be more than this. I had only to watch Alice to learn how.

My cat made me open the door.

Alice brought me into Creation. She showed me what I was missing by retreating from consciousness through denying my own death. In those hours on the deck with her on my lap, when I experienced Creation, I finally felt at peace with being alive.

Such a peace was not based on who I was or what I had done. It wasn't based on anything I had ever known. There was no basis to it, no reason I could invent. I simply felt at ease in the world. I was merely perceiving what was there. I was merely there. I just had to show up.

And once there, without any directive from me, as if a long dormant mechanism inside myself had snapped into operation, an appreciation of all that I could sense flowed through me.

My senses operated without judgment. They did not interpret what I was experiencing; they only sensed. But inside me, in my soul if that is what I can call it, my *Neshamah*, I felt an awe for this place I was in, an unutterable wonder at the presence of it, and this wonder seemed to radiate silently out of me like applause.

If I needed purpose, here it was. I had been avoiding my duty as a creature. I had not been noticing what had been created.

It wasn't scenery. It was just the back end of a house in the downtown of a city. The appreciation of Creation was not dependent upon human standards of beauty. I was in awe of being alive, this silent courage of energy that I was part of.

What had been a dilemma now made sense. It was a

practical matter. Previously I had been too afraid of death to allow myself to be conscious of being. Now I saw that if I were ever to be truly alive, I must admit the actuality of my own death. And after I had experienced Creation, once the famous veil had fallen away, I could see that it was worth the price of the ticket.

When I had paid the price, when I had faced up to the reality of death, both my own and of those I loved, when I had absorbed it into my life and accepted that I could never know or understand more than what was here, then I was able to hand in my ticket and step into Creation.

Death had no special power here; it was only part of the process of this ongoing energy. In Creation, death lost its horror and even grief melted away. For there are no comparisons here in Creation between possession and loss. There is only the moment and the spot, at this time and in this place.

To be in Creation is to be refreshed. It makes our situation manageable. If we take the time to just *be,* to put our minds back inside our bodies, our decaying, dying, evanescent bodies, and stop talking to ourselves for awhile, and feel the sweet sadness of this place, and go beyond the first loneliness of realizing that we are here, and then add Time to this spot—time, the machine that tells us that we are moving, that everything is happening now right here—then we are in Creation and we realize that creation has never stopped and we are part of it, both spectator and participant, and the fear becomes awe, and the world of human beings falls away and we are free.

And now the room you are in is not your prison. And each breath is a lifetime.

In any case, I will die. Perhaps, like Alice, I can die while I am in Creation. Better to have lived for at least some time in the awareness of the wonder and the strangeness of all this than to go to my death a slave of *Culture* and the tyranny of my own mind.

Alone, my mind would never have allowed me to get to Creation. I was too far gone. And the human world could no longer engage my attention.

So I watched my cat. I watched her move unfettered through time and space, how she peered at each moment as it passed and how she filled each spot with all the energies of her body. I ran my hand down her back and an electric spark of memory flowed into me to remind me of the place I am always in if I would only allow myself to be.

To be in Creation: the freedom of it! To be in the world as a living creature and know nothing but the duty to receive it and appreciate it! A cat's job!

27

Universe

We sailed through the universe together, a middle-aged man with a cat asleep on his lap: he, wrapped in winter coat and blanket, on a plastic patio chair in the December sunshine; and she, nestled in and heavy, sleeping for her life, sleeping away the pain and the terror of the pain and physical breakdown. And sailing through the universe in that place, in that moment, where there were the branch, the birds, her weight, our love, I burst the bubble, and I went out, and I WAS IN IT, the place where she always lived, the world, Creation, and I did not think backwards or forwards, so hours went by, not to move and disturb her, not to think of stiffness and cold,

but to allow myself at last to be being.

And the world has a calmness.

And a wonder beyond words.

And being alive has no analogy.

We can only praise the Creator.

And when we are truly in the world, being, just being, the praise comes freely, the awe like breath.

And then, the Kabbalah says, we are the senses of God, and the Creator views Creation.

This is our job. It's the Only Game in Town.

She brought me there. She saved my life.

28
The Cat's Hymn

And the cat sings: "Let everything that hath breath praise the Lord. Praise ye the Lord."

—*The Legends of the Jews*, Louis Ginzberg, The Jewish Publication Society, 1909.

29

Author's Note

What can I tell? All I know is that I had a cat and she woke me up and she made me open the door. I went out into the place I had always lived in but hadn't noticed. I probably would have died without noticing that I was living if I had not met her. I'm not in that place very often but I try to get there when I can. As the Talmud says:

You are not expected to finish the work.
Neither may you desist from it.

My cat reminds me.

30

Epilogue: Alice and the Deck

Sometimes I'm just reminded of my cat. A time comes when the memories are no longer sharp pains we wish would go away. They become hidden treasures that we're grateful to be able to hang on to, our inheritance from the dead; they live, somewhere. And an occurrence or conversation that passed by casually in the course of the joining of two lifetimes becomes a pivotal event in the focus of the lifetime left behind.

I remembered that Alice had taken me up to the deck once before, my body first. The mind followed later. Just one more story:

Most cats like to climb, but Alice, from the time she was a kitten, was a fanatic about it. Rocks, trees, fences, grapevines, bookshelves, ladders leaning absently against walls, up onto roofs, from roof to roof: she climbed anything.

I have always been terrified of heights. Standing near the railing of a balcony makes me woozy. Watching anyone else who is at an elevation higher than the floor makes me nervous. Seeing Alice climbing drove me crazy. I suspected she knew this.

The deck on the back of our house gave her plenty of opportunities to torment me. It had two levels: one off the second floor; and the other, up one level, connected by an outside stairway to the first. Alice was forever jumping up on the railing of the highest deck and prancing along that four-inch-wide piece of wood, three floors above the concrete sidewalk. It froze my blood. I would tiptoe over to her and quickly snatch her off. Eventually she knew I was going to do this and would slip out of my grasp at the last minute to race along the railing to another spot. To Alice it was a game and to me it was a near heart attack.

Somehow I knew that Alice was working on me, bringing me to the edge of my fears, presenting me with incidents of pure reality and shocking me awake. And in the end, she forced me through my fear.

It was the dead of winter after huge snowfalls and ice storms. I had come upstairs to the bathroom when I heard some plaintive mewing from somewhere. It sounded muffled yet nearby. I opened up some closets, expecting to see that Alice had been locked inside one of them accidentally, but they were empty of cat. The mewing continued and it was definitely coming from somewhere on the second floor.

Then it hit me. I rushed to the deck door. Through the glass, I could see Alice standing on the icy deck with her mouth round as a porthole, calling to me. Somehow she had climbed up the frozen grapevine to get here. This was her regular summer route; now she expected to come in the door.

The entrance was locked as usual for the season, but that was not the problem. The surface of the deck on the other side of it was covered in three inches of solid ice; you couldn't budge that door with a battering ram. Yet it was too slippery out there for Alice to climb back down. She was trapped on the deck and the only way off was through this door which was frozen shut solidly from the outside. Someone had to climb up to the deck and hack away the ice from in front of the entrance. And apparently that someone was me.

To make matters worse, there was no ladder in the house long enough to reach the first-level deck. The sole possible way of getting to the door was to climb up a TV tower antenna beside the house to the second-level deck, and then down the outside stairs to the first. That was a climb of three storeys up a tall triangle of aluminium tubing attached to the house by a few thin brackets. And the tubing was covered in ice.

First, I got really mad. Then I looked at Alice's frightened face and I got worried. She was freezing out there. I put on my coat and boots, grabbed a large screwdriver to hack away the ice in front of the door, and went out to the antenna. Here I got scared.

Fear of heights is not a rare problem but not easily understood by those who are unafflicted. Basically, I was convinced that if I climbed, I would fall. Therefore I generally avoided high places like diving boards, cliffs, and TV tower antennas. Now I had no choice.

A wind was swaying the antenna, rattling it against the side of the house. I grasped the tubing with my thick gloves, placed one large, clumsy winter boot on the bottom rung, and commenced my ascent.

I have little memory of what I thought about after the first nine or ten rungs. The old adage of not looking down came to mind and I began to treat each rung as a task in itself. (Actually, I did look down but I refused to comprehend what I was looking at.) The most alarming part was at the top when I had to climb over the second-level railing from the relative safety of my firm grip on the antenna. There was a moment when I would not let go. Then I heard Alice calling again. I scrambled over, stood on the top deck with all the muscles in my body as tight as a piano string, and wobbled my way down to the frozen door.

And there was my friend Alice, looking as if she had never expected anything else but that I would climb up three storeys to solve the problem of a door that wasn't open. I hacked away at the ice with the screwdriver, using a lot of my delayed fear as energy, and managed to get the entrance unblocked fairly quickly. When the door was open a crack, Alice shot inside. I followed, but a little more slowly, squeezing my body through like a tube of toothpaste. I was not about to go back the way I had come.

That spring, I had a door put in off the attic, giving easy access to the second-level deck. I wouldn't have to climb the antenna if Alice ever tried that stunt again.

She never did. Maybe that was one Cat School test that Alice figured I had passed with high enough marks. In any case, there were plenty of other assignments and demonstrations to come. We had a lot of ground to cover.

Acknowledgements

I would like to thank these friends for their encouragement and editorial suggestions. You may have no idea how much I appreciated and needed it.

Mary Jane Card, Jennifer Fisher,
Susan Harrison, Clare Coulter,
Madeleine Carstens, Susan Cody,
Semour Aronoff, Jim Colby, Jack Gewarter.

Any faults remaining in the manuscript are because I didn't listen.

For this first American edition, I would like to add special thanks to David Rosenberg for your kind support and advice; to Mark Labinger for making the connection; to Jeremy Tarcher and Joel Fotinos for your intelligence, enthusiasm, and respect for the text intact; and to the talented and industrious people of Tarcher/Putnam for doing such a great job.

If there are readers who wish to discuss or to comment on the book, you can contact me through the website at http://www.mycatsavedmylife.com or by writing to:

Phillip Schreibman
418 Ossington Avenue
Toronto, ON M6J 3A7
Canada